CRIMINAL PROFILING

Matt Anniss

Gareth Stevens
Publishing

Please visit our website, www.garethstevens.com. For a free color catalog of all our high-quality books, call toll free 1-800-542-2595 or fax 1-877-542-2596.

Library of Congress Cataloging-in-Publication Data

Anniss, Matt.
Criminal profiling / by Matt Anniss.
  p. cm. — (Crime science)
Includes index.
ISBN 978-1-4339-9481-4 (pbk.)
ISBN 978-1-4339-9482-1 (6-pack)
ISBN 978-1-4339-9480-7 (library binding)
1. Criminal behavior, Prediction of — Juvenile literature. 2. Criminal profilers — Juvenile literature. 3. Criminal investigation — Juvenile literature. I. Anniss, Matt. II. Title.
HV8073.5 A56 2014
363.25—dc23

First Edition

Published in 2014 by
Gareth Stevens Publishing
111 East 14th Street, Suite 349
New York, NY 10003

© 2014 Gareth Stevens Publishing

Produced by Calcium, www.calciumcreative.co.uk
Designed by Keith Williams and Paul Myerscough
Edited by Sarah Eason and Jennifer Sanderson

Photo credits: Cover: Shutterstock: Margarita Borodina bl, Grafvision br, Ivan101 tc, Andrew Lever c, Georg Preissl t. Inside: Dreamstime: Annieannie 26, Chrisjo88 20, Eddiesimages 32, Fotosmurf02 1, 36, Jank1000 11, Jeffbanke 28, Martinmark 18, Miluxian 24, Rmwood 21, Rtimages 31, Showface 29, Starletdarlene 34, Trekandshoot 13; Shutterstock: Andrey Popov 10, Yuri Arcurs 40, Anthony Berenyi 38, Tyler Boyes 12, Kevin L Chesson 37, Corepics VOF 4, 17, Shawn Hempel 27, iQoncept 22, Denise Kappa 8, Mangostock 14, MaxyM 9, Mikeledray 45, Miker 15, Monkey Business Images 5, Nomad Soul 39, Rossco 23, Lisa S. 42, Simon G 43, Spirit of America 41, StockLite 25, Graham Taylor 16, Anatoly Tiplyashin 19, TX King 6, Wavebreakmedia 7, WilleeCole 44; United States Department of Justice 35b; Wikipedia: FBI Photos 33, German Federal Archives 30b, Dan Huse 35t.

Printed in the United States of America

CPSIA compliance information: Batch #CS13GS: For further information contact Gareth Stevens, New York, New York at 1-800-542-2595.

CRIME SCIENCE

CONTENTS

CRIME PROFILING

Tracking and catching criminals can be a difficult business. Although the police have many scientific methods of collecting and analyzing evidence, sometimes these are not enough to crack a case. This is why the science of crime profiling is so important.

New Science

Crime profiling is one of the newest methods in crime science. Crime profilers study where, when, and why crimes are committed. By doing this, crime profilers can learn a lot about who may have carried out a crime, and why it was committed. Some crime profilers are experts in the way criminals think, while others specialize in spotting patterns in where crimes take place. Some advise the police about how to reduce crime, while others are brought in to help catch dangerous criminals.

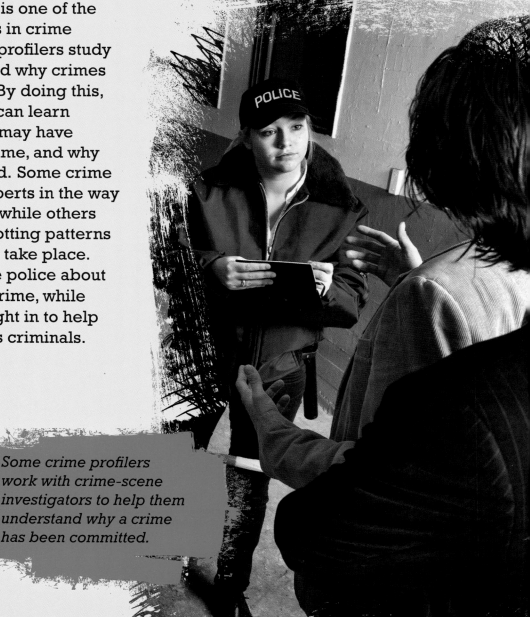

Some crime profilers work with crime-scene investigators to help them understand why a crime has been committed.

Study and Research

The various methods used by crime profilers are based on study and research, rather than traditional police work. Although many of the techniques have been tried, tested, and proven to work, others are based on what researchers call theories. A theory is an idea, backed up with a solid argument based on detailed study. Many scientific theories have changed the way we view the world, while others have later been proven to be incorrect. In the world of crime profiling, theories are constantly changing.

BACK IN THE LAB

Crime profilers of the future all start out by attending universities. There, they study a science called criminology, which is the basis of all crime-profiling work. Universities play a huge role in crime profiling; it is the research carried out there that often forms the basis of crime-profiling methods.

Many would-be profilers attend college to learn the skills they need to help the police catch dangerous criminals.

CHAPTER ONE
CRIMINOLOGY

The basis of all crime profiling is criminology. This is the scientific study of crime. Many crime profiling techniques used by the police are based on criminology.

Criminology for Beginners

Criminology is not a new science. The term was first used by an Italian lawyer and university professor named Raffaele Garofalo in 1885. However, over the last 100 years, criminology has developed into a vast subject with many different ideas and theories.

Criminologists

People who study criminology are known as criminologists. It is their job to look at where and how frequently crimes take place, and why criminals break the law.

Some criminologists spend time talking to prisoners to try to find out why they turned to crime.

The Causes of Crime

Some criminologists look in detail at the things that influence criminal behavior, such as the world around us, where we live, and how much money we have. Others specialize in specific forms of crime. Criminologists study every aspect of crime in order to try to explain why it happens, and more importantly, how it can be stopped.

CRACKED

One of the oldest ideas in criminology is Rational Choice Theory. This is the idea that criminals make a conscious choice to commit crimes. Supporters of this theory say that the way to deter people from choosing to commit crimes is to offer tougher punishments.

Contrasting Ideas

Because criminology is such a broad science, criminologists often disagree on the causes of crime. Over the years, many different theories have been put forward to explain criminal behavior. This is a natural part of science. New evidence may prove old theories to be incorrect, while scientists often disagree about what the evidence tells us. Theories are just ideas—it is how they are used in the fight against crime that is important.

Criminology can be a difficult subject to study because many of its theories contradict each other.

DIFFERENT THEORIES

Over the years, criminologists have put forward many different ideas to explain the causes of crime. Some are controversial, and others have been changed and adapted over time.

Choosing Crime

Criminologists have long argued over the causes of crime. The very first criminologists, known as the "Classical School of Criminology," believed that people choose to become criminals.

Developing Theories

Later, criminologists of the "Positivist School" argued that people turn to crime due to forces beyond their control, such as losing their job, knowing other criminals, or living in run-down areas. In the early twentieth century, "Chicago School" criminologists expanded on this idea. They believed that being poor and not doing well at school were two of the greatest causes of crime.

Some criminologists believe that having more police officers on the streets deters criminal behavior.

POLICE

Many criminologists think that poor people are more likely to commit crimes than wealthy people.

Criminal Ideas

Since the early twentieth century, countless theories have been put forward to explain why people turn to crime. Some criminologists believe that certain people have a "criminal mind" and are therefore more likely to do terrible things. Other schools of thought believe that children inherit "criminal traits" from their parents.

Attitudes and Desire

Over time, attitudes toward certain crimes have changed, so people may not believe, or care, that they are breaking the law when committing these crimes. For instance, some criminologists argue that crime has increased because people are willing to break the law to get the latest must-have clothes and gadgets.

CRACKED

Criminologists have developed an idea called "Strain Theory." They argue that when money is tight, jobs are hard to come by, and people feel pressured by the strain of day-to-day life, they are more likely to turn to crime as a way out of their problems.

VICTIMOLOGY

One of the latest ideas in criminology theory is victimology. This is the study of victims of crime, how the crime affects them, and whether their actions put them at risk of attack.

Controversial Ideas

Some of the ideas put forward by victimologists are highly controversial. One theory is that some people are more likely to become victims of crime because of certain things they do. This could be doing a specific type of high-risk job, walking alone late at night, or being particularly friendly to strangers. This is a very unpopular idea because it suggests that victims of crime make themselves a target for criminals.

Victimologists often talk to victims of crime to find out how they have been affected.

Following a high-profile crime, the victims often find themselves in demand by television news journalists.

Positive Steps

Victimology includes studying how people are affected by the crimes committed against them. By doing this, the police, courts of law, and governments can understand more about how people feel about crime, and what punishments should be given to criminals.

Victims' Rights

Today, more consideration is given to the rights of victims of crime. In the United States, victims are encouraged to go to court to explain how a crime has affected them. They are allowed to speak before the judge decides on the punishment of a convicted criminal.

BACK IN THE LAB

Some victimologists are employed by the government to study what effect crime has on victims, and how the legal system can make victims' lives more bearable. Others study crime data to try to figure out what sorts of people are more likely to be the victims of crime.

ENVIRONMENTAL CRIMINOLOGY

Many criminologists believe that the way people behave is influenced by their surroundings. They think that there is a direct link between where people live and whether they commit crimes.

Poverty Means Crime

There is a close link between crime levels—how many crimes happen—and poverty. More crimes happen in poor areas of cities. While some criminologists think that this is because there are fewer people with jobs and money is tight in these areas, environmental criminologists believe that the condition of buildings, the number of boarded-up properties, and how many parks and open spaces are present are just as important.

Trees Are Good

Some environmental criminologists think that the number of trees in an area has an effect on the crime rate. Research in Portland, Oregon, proved that levels of crime are significantly lower in areas where there are more large trees.

Environmental criminologists think that building wider streets, surrounded by trees, helps to reduce crime levels.

Building a Safer Community

Studies by environmental criminologists have also suggested that the height of backyard fences, the size and shape of windows, and the sort of street lighting used can also have an effect on crime rates. Because of this, town planners and architects have begun working with environmental criminologists when designing buildings and housing estates. They hope that by doing this, they will deter criminals from targeting these houses and the people who live there.

CRACKED

The idea of trying to reduce crime through the design of buildings and neighborhoods is called Crime Prevention Through Environmental Design (CPTED). Ideas regularly used by CPTED specialists include widening sidewalks to encourage more people to walk and bicycle around, adding trees to public areas, installing surveillance cameras, and making street lighting much brighter.

A neighborhood with plenty of trees and green spaces is less likely to be targeted by criminals than a built-up inner-city neighborhood.

13

CHAPTER TWO
CRIME ANALYSIS

Although criminology theories are the basis of all crime profiling, they do not always have a great deal of practical use for tackling crime. The same cannot be said of crime analysis, an area of criminal science that has revolutionized police work in the twenty-first century.

Practical Purpose

Crime analysis is examining all the available information about crimes in order to identify and predict trends. Police forces must record information about every crime reported, including where it was, who the victim was, and what sort of crime took place.

This information is stored on vast banks of computers and it is of great use to crime analysts. Not only can they use it to work out crime rates (the number of crimes that happen every week, month, or year), but they can also pinpoint exactly where crimes are taking place.

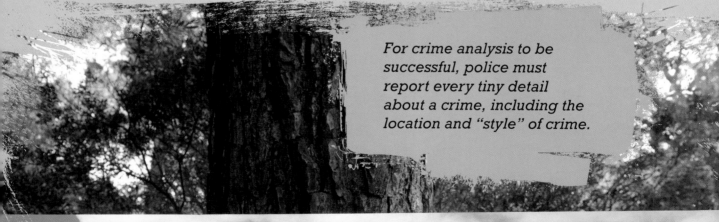

For crime analysis to be successful, police must report every tiny detail about a crime, including the location and "style" of crime.

ROSS **POLICE LINE DO NOT CROSS**

A greater police presence is often seen in areas where high-tech crime analysis of criminal activity has taken place.

Useful Information

Police forces all over the world use crime analysts to help them police the streets more effectively. If they know where, when, and what sort of crimes take place, then they can try to reduce crime. For example, if they know that there are more street crimes at night in a particular area, they can send out more police patrols at night to deter criminals. If the statistics show that drug users commit a lot of crimes, then they can put more resources into trying to catch drug dealers.

CRACKED

Crime analysts are often people who are really good at math. Every day, they have to trawl through software programs full of numbers and statistics to try to find trends. A trend is a pattern—for example, a rise in violent crime or a reduction in the number of teenagers committing crimes.

15

SOFTWARE AND STATISTICS

Crime analysis is a complicated process, but one that is changing the way the police tackle crimes. Using specially designed computer software, analysts can track the location, type, and frequency of crimes committed.

NYPD's Big Idea

The New York Police Department (NYPD) pioneered the use of crime analysis. In 1994, the NYPD started using a system called CompStat. CompStat used computer software to compile reports of all the crime committed in New York City.

CompStat

NYPD software allowed crime analysts to view maps of the city, which showed the location of the crimes. The system also included data on the police response, such as how many officers were sent to a crime scene. As part of the process, representatives from each of the city's 76 area precincts met to go through the crime-analysis information.

Special computer software allows police forces to track and log details of where crimes have happened.

CompStat has helped police forces around the world to find, arrest, and lock up many criminals.

Cutting Crime

CompStat is a huge success. According to NYPD officials, it has helped cut crime in the city dramatically. It also played an important role in cutting the number of murders from more than 1,100 in 1995 to 414 in 2012. Because of the system's success, it has since been adopted by police forces all over the United States, Canada, and the United Kingdom. By knowing all of the facts about where, when, and how often crimes happen, the police can more accurately manage their response to reported crimes.

CRACKED

Some police forces in the United States, Canada, and the United Kingdom have started allowing the public to see the location and details of crimes collected using the CompStat process. Using the website www.crimereports.com, you can get updates of where, when, and what sort of crimes are being reported.

SOLVING PROBLEMS

Crime analysis is now being used by police forces to identify the biggest crime problems in their area, so that they can tackle them head-on. This approach is called "problem-oriented policing."

Problem-Oriented Policing

Professor Herman Goldstein of the University of Wisconsin-Madison invented problem-oriented policing. Goldstein suggested to police forces that they combine crime analysis reports with the thoughts of police officers on the ground.

Treating the Root

In problem-oriented policing, officers are encouraged to use systems such as CompStat to spot crime trends (see pages 16–17). For example, by observing a rise in vandals breaking windows or convenience-store robberies, they may more easily find the cause of the crimes. By dealing with the root of the problem, the number of crimes of that type should drop dramatically.

Problem-oriented policing has been successfully used to cut down car crime in a number of US cities.

People Power

Most police forces that use problem-oriented policing try to involve the public. They actively encourage people to tell them about the problems in their area, often by holding weekly community meetings. In most areas where problem-oriented policing has been used, crime rates have dropped and confidence in the police has risen. When relations between the police and the public are at their best, crime is most likely to drop. After first being tested out in Wisconsin, problem-oriented policing has since been used in the United States in Maryland, New Jersey, North Carolina, and California, as well as in the United Kingdom.

REAL-LIFE CASE

Police in San Diego have used the problem-oriented policing approach to cut down drug dealing in an 80-unit apartment complex. After talking to residents and the apartment block's manager, they were able to identify the drug dealers and users and either arrest them or evict them from their homes. The drug dealing stopped almost overnight.

By talking to the public about the crime problems in their area, police can gain vital information about criminal patterns in a particular place.

CHAPTER THREE

GEOGRAPHIC PROFILING

Geographic profiling is the "where" of modern policing. It uses advanced software to look at where crime is happening, either to identify patterns of criminal behavior or to help solve serious cases, such as serial killings or chains of robberies.

Where and Why

Geographic profiling is concerned with two things—where and why crimes take place. It is based on the old idea of crime mapping. In crime mapping, detectives would stick pins into a large map to see if there were any patterns between crime scenes and where evidence had been found.

Familiar Ground

Geographic profilers suggest that most criminals will commit their crimes in an area they know well. This could be close to where they live, an area in which they work, or somewhere they regularly go in their free time. Geographic profiling is most often used to help police with crimes that may be connected.

Geographic profiling has helped police to track down criminals, such as burglars and muggers who commit crimes in a small area.

Arson, a crime in which someone deliberately starts fires, is an area that has been targeted by geographic profilers.

Crime Patterns

Geographic profilers are specialists in spotting what they call "patterns of offender behavior." For example, if a serial killer was at large and all of the victims had been found close to bars, it would suggest that he or she picked them at random when out at night. In cases of serial crimes, such as murders or arson, more often than not there are patterns in the way criminals behave. These patterns are not always obvious, so geographic profiling can help find the criminal.

REAL-LIFE CASE

Geographic profiling was first used in 1981, during the hunt for a British serial killer nicknamed the "Yorkshire Ripper." A forensics and mapping expert named Stuart Kind told the police that he believed the killer lived in one of two small villages. When the Ripper, Peter Sutcliffe, was arrested two weeks later, Kind was proved right.

CRIME MAPPING

The backbone of geographical profiling is crime mapping. Although now quite advanced, thanks to the use of computers, it has been used by police forces for many years for a number of reasons.

Pins in a Map

In the early days of crime mapping, police stuck pins into large maps. Originally, crime mapping was used in serious cases with multiple crimes to help narrow down the search for evidence. By looking at the location of the pins in the map, police could identify the best areas to look for clues.

Geographic Information Systems

In recent years, crime mapping has become much more sophisticated. Today's crime analysts use a type of computer software called Geographic Information Systems (GIS) to keep track of the location of crimes, spot trends, and advise police about crime hotspots.

Maps created using crime data help the police to find out which neighborhoods are the least safe. On this map of the United States, the areas shown in dark orange have the highest level of violent crimes.

CRACKED

Crime analysts who use crime mapping spend a lot of their time comparing many different types of information. In order to guide the police, they will compile presentations showing the exact location of specific crimes over a set period of time, the locations of certain types of crime, and how the police responded.

"Real time" crime-mapping information is used by police forces when deciding where to send officers.

Advanced Mapping

The GIS used by crime analysts allows them to look at many different types of information. They can, for example, compare the location of crimes with the locations of schools, betting establishments, bars, nightclubs, and housing areas. Doing this can help them understand the underlying causes of crime, and in turn suggest solutions to the problems. Crime mapping is a vital part of the CompStat system used by many police forces (see pages 16–17), and it has also been used to assist problem-oriented policing projects (see pages 18–19).

23

SOFTWARE SOLUTIONS

The days of sticking pins in maps mounted on the walls of police stations are long gone. Today, crime mapping and geographic profiling is carried out using advanced computer software programs.

Computer Assistance

Modern crime-mapping software is based on GIS (see page 22). These advanced computer programs combine mapping software with databases. A database is a program that allows users to store and search through huge amounts of information quickly and easily.

GIS Software

Using GIS software, crime analysts can search for information, which will then be displayed on a map or series of maps. The first-ever specialist geographic-profiling computer program was developed by Canada's Dr. Kim Rossmo. It was designed to help solve serial murder cases.

Today, old-fashioned paper maps have been replaced by high-tech computer systems to accurately mark where crimes have taken place.

The information stored in geographical-profiling and crime-mapping computer programs can be displayed as graphs and charts.

Leading Systems

There are now a number of specialist geographic-profiling software systems available to crime analysts. One of these is called Rigel Analyst. According to its makers, this program has a high success rate and can narrow down the likely home of a wanted criminal. They say it is 95 percent accurate. This means that it is correct in 95 out of 100 crimes. Another popular program used by many police forces is CrimeStat. This has features similar to Rigel Analyst, but can also help analysts figure out how far criminals travel to carry out their crimes.

BACK IN THE LAB

When hunting for serial killers, many police forces use a geographic-profiling progam called Gemini. Gemini has been designed specifically to figure out which crimes may belong to a series or are the work of the same criminal. It even ranks crimes in order of how likely they are to be part of a series.

25

THE CONS OF GEOGRAPHIC PROFILING

Although popular, geographic profiling is not always as successful as other profiling methods. According to critics of the theory, this is because it has serious limitations.

Limited Use

The biggest problem with geographic profiling is that it is concerned only with the locations of crimes. While some criminals may carry out their crimes in a certain area or in a pattern, this is not always the case. If detectives base their investigations on geographic-profile findings that turn out to be wrong, they will have wasted a lot of time and money. What is more, in that time, the criminal would be free to continue to carry out even more crimes.

Many Areas, One Criminal

Often geographic-profiling systems also overlook the fact that some criminals are prepared to travel large distances to carry out their crimes. If a serial killer murdered his or her victims in several areas or states, geographical profiling would be of little use.

Geographic profilers do not take into account the fact that some criminals commit crimes in several areas.

Rather than analyzing a crime scene, geographical profilers study where crimes have taken place, rather than how and why they occurred.

Software Issues

The third worry that critics have is about the computer software itself. The results of geographic profiling will only ever be as good as the software being used and the information that is entered into the database. If the information is out of date, incorrect, or even misleading, the geographic profile will be inaccurate.

Use with Caution

Critics say that although geographic profiling can be a useful tool in serious crime cases, it should only ever be used with other methods, such as evidence gathering and interviewing witnesses.

REAL-LIFE CASE

Despite its limitations, geographic profiling does get results. In 2005, Raymond Lopez was arrested for robbing more than 200 houses in Orange County, California, after police used geographic-profiling software to predict where he lived. More police were sent to the area, leading to Lopez's arrest.

27

CHAPTER FOUR
OFFENDER PROFILING

The best-known area of crime profiling is offender profiling. Also known as psychological profiling, offender profiling has been featured in many movies and television series.

Who and Why

Offender profiling is the process of trying to figure out who committed a crime and why they did it, based on an understanding of criminal behavior. Offender profilers try to identify criminals by analyzing the crime, how it was committed, and any other relevant case evidence.

Studying the Clues

Criminals may leave clues at the crime scene about the type of person they are and how they think. Offender profilers also look in close detail at the choices criminals make before and after a crime, such as how well it was planned and the methods used to carry out the crime. These can also offer clues about the type of people they are.

Unlike geographic profiling, offender profiling is based on the careful examination of all case evidence.

SHERIFF'S LINE DO NOT CROSS

Criminal profilers examine case evidence carefully in order to find clues about the criminal's identity.

BACK IN THE LAB

Offender profilers divide their time between studying case evidence in order to create psychological profiles, teaching police detectives about basic profiling techniques, and learning more about how and why crimes are committed. They spend most of their time in an office and rarely visit crime scenes.

Human Behavior

Offender profilers often start out their career as psychologists. These are scientists who specialize in human behavior. They do not work on all cases and, in general, the police use them only to help catch very serious criminals. To help police, they must create a detailed description of the sort of person who may have committed the crime.

Patience and Knowledge

Offender profiling can be a tricky and time-consuming business, but if a criminal is caught, it is very rewarding. Offender profiling requires patience, an understanding of criminal behavior, and a knowledge of personality types (for example, whether someone is outgoing or introverted).

THE HISTORY OF OFFENDER PROFILING

The psychological profiling of criminals is not a new development. It has been used in different forms since the nineteenth century. Over the years, a number of famous profilers have helped develop the science behind the technique.

Jack the Ripper

The first offender profiler was a British doctor named Thomas Bond. During the 1880s, he studied the crimes of a famous murderer nicknamed "Jack the Ripper." After looking in detail at the Ripper's crimes, he worked out that the killer was likely to be a quiet, middle-aged man who was "strong, composed, and daring."

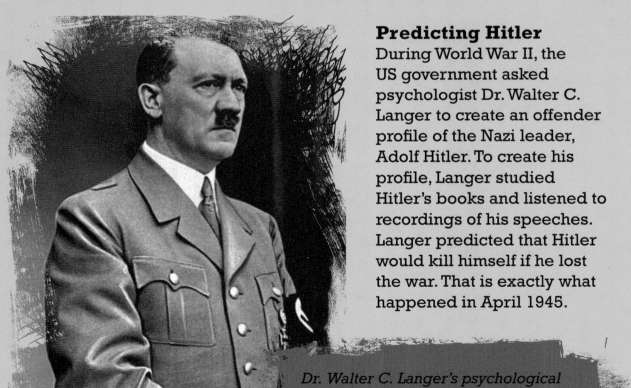

Predicting Hitler

During World War II, the US government asked psychologist Dr. Walter C. Langer to create an offender profile of the Nazi leader, Adolf Hitler. To create his profile, Langer studied Hitler's books and listened to recordings of his speeches. Langer predicted that Hitler would kill himself if he lost the war. That is exactly what happened in April 1945.

Dr. Walter C. Langer's psychological profile of Adolf Hitler was crucial in helping the Allies to win World War II.

Bomb Squad

In the 1950s, a psychologist named James A. Brussel helped police to track down a terrorist who had planted bombs in New York City over a 16-year period. Brussel studied the case files and figured out that the bomber was likely to be a "heavy" middle-aged mechanic who once worked for the Consolidated Edison power company. The description helped the police to catch George Metesky, whose appearance and background accurately matched Brussel's profile. The case inspired the FBI to take the technique more seriously.

FBI psychological profilers work closely with detectives while investigating murder cases.

REAL-LIFE CASE

Offender profiling helped the FBI to track down one of the United States' most dangerous serial killers, Ted Bundy. Offender profiling specialist Dr. Richard B. Jarvis provided police with a description that accurately predicted Bundy's age, characteristics, and above-average intelligence.

THE FBI METHOD

In the United States, offender profiling is carried out using a special five-phase technique called the FBI profiling method. This was developed by two of the fathers of modern offender profiling, John E. Douglas and Robert Ressler.

Stage One

The FBI profiling method uses five different stages to create an accurate profile of a dangerous criminal, usually a murderer. First, profilers examine all available case information and evidence, from crime-scene photos and victim profiles to police reports and witness statements. This is known as the "assimilation stage."

Stage Two

The second stage is called the "classification stage." In this stage, profilers decide whether the criminal is organized or disorganized. Organized criminals often plan their crimes in detail, while disorganized criminals usually do not plan attacks and often leave lots of evidence.

During the "assimilation stage," profilers carefully study all case evidence from a crime scene in detail.

Students at the FBI Academy are taught the techniques behind the world-famous FBI profiling method.

Before and After

In the third stage, profilers focus on the criminal's behavior before and after the crime. The idea is to try to figure out the exact sequence of events in order to learn not only how the crime was committed, but also what it says about the criminal's personality. When that is complete, the profilers look for the criminal's "signature." This is anything the criminal does at the scene of the crime that is different or unusual and may give a clue about the way he or she thinks. The final stage of the FBI method is to create a profile for detectives to use.

CRACKED

John E. Douglas is one of the most successful FBI criminal psychologists of all time. During the 1970s, he worked at the FBI's Behavioral Sciences Unit, where he taught his famous FBI method of profiling. He retired in 1995, but is still asked by police forces to help in the hunt for serial killers.

THE BEHAVIOR ANALYSIS UNIT

The FBI has a special department dedicated to psychological analysis and offender profiling. It is part of the National Center for the Analysis of Violent Crime (NCAVC), and it is called the Behavior Analysis Unit (BAU).

BAU

The BAU came into being in the 1970s, after the successful launch of Robert Ressler's Behavioral Sciences Unit. The Unit is based in Virginia and takes responsibility for most offender profiling undertaken by the FBI.

Handy Help

When police forces and FBI departments are hunting killers or other dangerous criminals, they often contact the BAU for help. Sometimes, the BAU sends profilers around the country to help investigators. At other times they offer advice over the telephone. They also offer training for FBI agents in the basic principles of offender profiling.

Profilers from the BAU are regularly asked by detectives investigating serious cases to go to crime scenes.

Television shows such as *Criminal Minds* are watched by millions of viewers. Actor Thomas Gibson plays Aaron Hotchner, the Unit Chief of the BAU.

Investigative Analysis

The BAU specializes in "criminal investigative analysis." Criminal investigative analysis involves looking closely at serious crime, criminal behavior, and also the investigation itself to help detectives crack difficult cases. The Unit carries out its tasks using a number of different methods, from offender profiling and traditional crime analysis to advising detectives on how best to manage manhunts for serial killers.

One of the ways in which BAU profilers use their knowledge of criminal behavior is to advise detectives on what to ask suspected criminals during police interviews. They devise a series of questions that are most likely to result in a confession from the criminal.

Specialist Staff

Most of the Unit's staff members are experienced criminal profilers specializing in violent crimes such as murder, crimes against children, or terrorism. The Unit's scientific approach and great knowledge of criminal behavior has helped bring many dangerous criminals to justice over the last 20 years.

35

LINKAGE ANALYSIS

One of the tasks often performed by BAU crime profilers is linkage analysis. This technique brings together elements of criminal and geographic profiling to figure out if a series of crimes is linked.

Connected Events

Linkage analysis is a method used by profilers and police detectives to figure out whether a series of crimes was committed by the same criminal. For example, police could be investigating a series of killings in different states that was carried out over a long period of time. They may not look like they are connected, but by carrying out detailed linkage analysis, criminal profilers may be able to prove that they were the work of the same criminal. When carrying out linkage analysis, criminal profilers will try to use their understanding of criminal behavior to spot patterns that link the crimes together.

Crime-scene evidence that looks out of place could link a crime to others that have previously happened in other areas of the country.

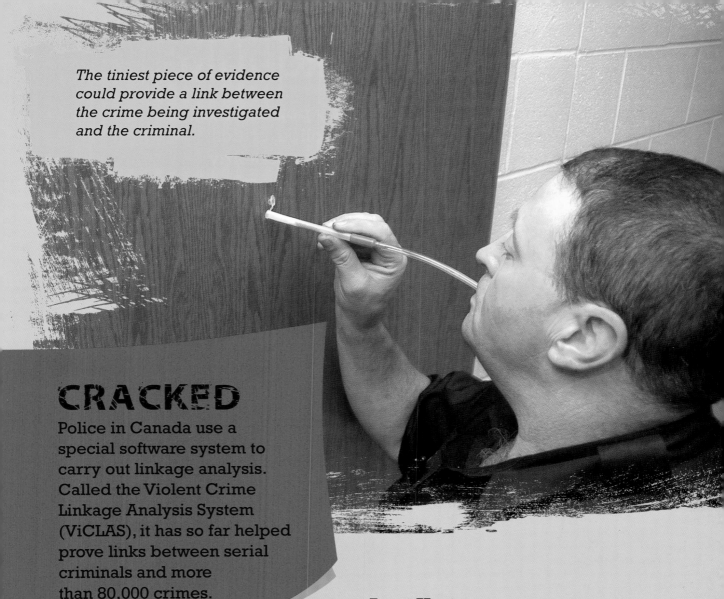

The tiniest piece of evidence could provide a link between the crime being investigated and the criminal.

CRACKED

Police in Canada use a special software system to carry out linkage analysis. Called the Violent Crime Linkage Analysis System (ViCLAS), it has so far helped prove links between serial criminals and more than 80,000 crimes.

Clues in Maps

Today, linkage analysts will often carry out geographic profiling as part of the process. This is to see whether there are additional links or clues in the location of the crimes or where bodies were discovered in murder cases.

Last Hope

Generally, linkage analysis is a last resort for detectives working on murder cases. It is used only in rare cases where evidence is limited. Often, crimes are solved using DNA evidence, which can provide clues about a criminal's identity, or fingerprint marks left at the crime scene. When this type of evidence does not exist, detectives may turn to linkage analysis.

37

PROBLEMS WITH PROFILING

Although offender profiling is hugely popular with the public and is often used by the police, critics say it is not very reliable. They say it is not nearly scientific enough, and when profiles prove to be incorrect, it can waste valuable police time.

Mistakes

The biggest problems with offender profiling happen when profilers make mistakes. If they assess all the evidence and tell police to look for a particular type of person, more often than not, detectives will put great faith in their opinion. If the profile turns out to be incorrect, the police will be searching for the wrong person and may even arrest someone who is totally blameless. This happened in 1996, when security guard Richard Jewell was arrested for bombing Centennial Park in Atlanta during the Olympic Games. Jewell's arrest gave the real bomber, Eric Rudolph, time to carry out two more bomb attacks.

The incorrect arrest of Richard Jewell for the Centennial Park bombings in Atlanta proved that offender profiling does not always work.

Critics of offender profiling say that it can lead to innocent people being arrested for crimes they did not commit.

Not Enough Science

Critics of offender profiling say that it is impossible to draw conclusions about somebody's personality, background, and appearance from what they do when committing a crime. They argue that detectives should not read too much into the way someone behaves before and after they have committed a crime, because they may be acting differently due to the pressure of the situation.

CHAPTER FIVE
INTO THE FUTURE

As a new science, crime profiling is by no means perfect. However, every year it is growing in popularity, with new ideas being put forward and techniques being developed.

Problems to Solve

All of the methods, techniques, ideas, and theories of offender profiling have good and bad points. Criminologists and crime profilers understand this and are working hard to increase their understanding of criminals, their behavior, and the science of catching them.

By comparing crime trends and statistics from different parts of the world, criminologists hope that they can learn more about the causes of crime.

Compare and Contrast

One of the latest developments in criminology is the idea of comparative criminology. This is the study of crime across different countries and groups of people (for example, those who earn a certain amount of money or follow a certain religion). The idea is to try to identify differences and similarities between crime rates and types of crime. By doing this, criminologists may be able to figure out the major causes of crime and how they could be tackled in the future.

Leading criminologists believe the best way to cut crime would be to improve the lives of those living in poor areas.

Crime Prevention

One idea that has gained popularity in recent years is crime prevention as a way of lowering crime rates. The idea is to stop, or prevent, people from turning to crime in the first place. Many criminologists have spent years studying which approaches work.

Tackling Poverty

In 2004, some of the world's leading criminologists put together a report listing the best ways to prevent crime. They suggested that countries should work together to tackle the global drug trade and focus more on the problems that cause crime, such as poverty.

Some of the busiest crime profilers are forensic psychiatrists. These are scientists with a deep knowledge of how the human mind works. They are often used in court cases to pass judgment on whether or not criminals have any mental illnesses that may make them act differently.

INVESTIGATIVE PSYCHOLOGY

New, cutting-edge scientific techniques are being developed all the time to help crime profilers do their job. One of the latest is investigative psychology.

Research Is Key

Investigative psychologists, so-called because they investigate with methods that are similar to those used by detectives, are not unlike offender profilers. However, they take a much more scientific approach. Investigative psychologists try to help police by basing their conclusions on scientific research, rather than their own experiences of criminal behavior.

Different Approach

Investigative psychology differs from the FBI method of profiling, which asks criminal profilers to "think like the criminal." Investigative psychologists may assist the police with their work but spend most of their time carrying out research and studying case evidence and human behavior.

Investigative psychologists study all aspects of human behavior in order to figure out why people commit crimes such as burglary.

Investigative psychology has helped many countries solve homicides.

Finding Patterns

Some of the techniques used by investigative psychologists are similar to those used by crime analysts. They are just as interested in numbers as they are in the way people think. They want to try to prove links between patterns of behavior found in violent criminals, such as being aggressive, and how they carry out their crimes.

The Importance of Research

Investigative psychologists think that by carrying out detailed research, they will create much more accurate offender profiles in the future. Leading investigative psychologists believe that in the future they will understand far more about criminal behavior than regular crime profilers.

CRACKED

The South African Police Service (SAPS) was one of the first police forces to set up an investigative psychology unit. The South African Investigative Psychology Section was set up in 1996 to help detectives solve crimes using both detailed research and crime-stopping experience.

YOUNG SCIENCE

In the last 30 years, crime profiling has gone from an experimental technique to one of the cornerstones of modern policing. It has revolutionized the way crimes are investigated.

Modern Science

Crime mapping helps police forces to cut down crime and better plan their response to urgent calls from the public. Geographic profiling has helped detectives to pinpoint the whereabouts of many violent criminals, murderers, and arsonists.

Thanks to psychological offender profiling, detectives now better understand the way criminals behave and how they may think. Crime analysis allows police to quickly spot crime trends, while problem-oriented policing has improved many lives by cutting crime.

Although it is a young science, criminal profiling has helped to catch and convict dangerous criminals.

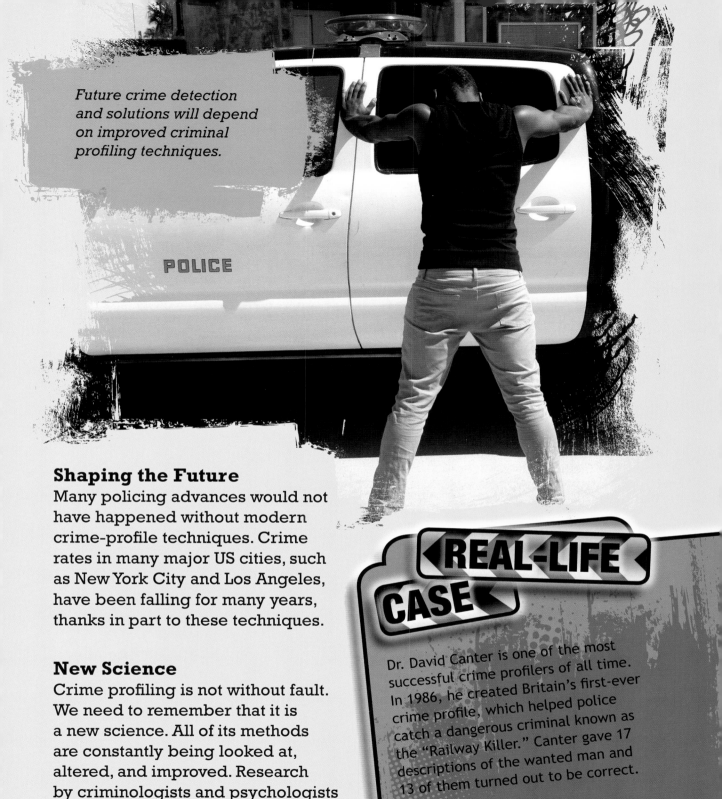

Future crime detection and solutions will depend on improved criminal profiling techniques.

Shaping the Future

Many policing advances would not have happened without modern crime-profile techniques. Crime rates in many major US cities, such as New York City and Los Angeles, have been falling for many years, thanks in part to these techniques.

New Science

Crime profiling is not without fault. We need to remember that it is a new science. All of its methods are constantly being looked at, altered, and improved. Research by criminologists and psychologists will help shape the future of all detective work. Policing mistakes may still be made, but far more criminals will be caught.

REAL-LIFE CASE

Dr. David Canter is one of the most successful crime profilers of all time. In 1986, he created Britain's first-ever crime profile, which helped police catch a dangerous criminal known as the "Railway Killer." Canter gave 17 descriptions of the wanted man and 13 of them turned out to be correct.

45

GLOSSARY

adapted changed

analysis a detailed study of something

architect somebody who designs buildings for a living

arson deliberately setting fire to things

attitude how someone thinks about something

committed carried out a crime

controversial something that is unpopular or goes against popular thinking

convicted criminal somebody who has been judged guilty of a crime by a court of law

crime rates also called crime levels, these are statistics used by the police to show whether the number of crimes in a town or city have gone up or down

criminology the scientific study of crime

data information

database a computer software program for storing and sorting information

deter to put off

evidence something that proves an idea right or wrong, or (in criminal cases) that proves that somebody is guilty of something

experts people who know a lot about a certain subject

FBI short for the Federal Bureau of Investigation, a government agency belonging to the United States Department of Justice

manhunt an extensive search for a criminal

offender a criminal

research looking into something in great detail in order to learn more about it

resources any money, people, or equipment that can be used by an organization (for example, the police)

revolutionized dramatically changed

serial a series of connected crimes (for example, robberies, or a sequence of events)

serial killer someone who has killed a number of people

software program something on a computer designed to do a particular task, such as send e-mail, look at the Internet, or play games

statistics facts based on numbers, usually arrived at after collecting information or carrying out research. Crime rates are usually presented as statistics.

surveillance watching, looking, or listening, using cameras and other recording equipment

theory an idea backed up by evidence, usually based on research

vandals criminals who damage things on purpose (for example, windows, houses, or cars)

victim someone who has a crime committed against them (for example, somebody who has been attacked or robbed)

FOR MORE INFORMATION

BOOKS

Brown, Jeremy. *Crime Files: Four-Minute Forensic Mysteries.*
New York, NY: Scholastic, 2006.

Beres, D. B., and Anna Prokos. *Crime Scene: Profilers and Poison.*
New York, NY: Scholastic, 2009.

King, Colin. *Detective's Handbook.* London, UK: Usborne, 2008.

Levy, Janey. *Careers in Criminal Profiling.* New York, NY:
Rosen Central, 2009.

WEBSITES

Find out what a criminal profiler does and how you could take up a career in criminology at:
**www.criminologycareers.about.com/od/Career_Profiles/a/
Criminal-Profiler.htm**

Read more about crime mapping and its usefulness to the police at:
www.gislounge.com/crime-mapping-gis-goes-mainstream/

Find out what happens at a crime scene investigation and how specialists such as crime profilers assist investigations at:
www.howstuffworks.com/csi.htm

Publisher's note to educators and parents: Our editors have carefully reviewed these websites to ensure that they are suitable for students. Many websites change frequently, however, and we cannot guarantee that a site's future contents will continue to meet our high standards of quality and educational value. Be advised that students should be closely supervised whenever they access the Internet.

INDEX